MONSTER MANIA

BEASTLY MONSTERS

FROM DRAGONS TO GRIFFINS

KATIE MARSICO

LERNER PUBLICATIONS ◆ MINNEAPOLIS

To Jack and Anthony Sebastian

Lerner Publications
A division of Lerner Publishing Group, Inc.
241 First Avenue North
Minneapolis, MN 55401 USA

For reading levels and more information, look up this title at www.lernerbooks.com.

Main body text set in Adrianna Regular 15/19.
Typeface provided by Chank.

Library of Congress Cataloging-in-Publication Data

Names: Marsico, Katie, 1980– author.
Title: Beastly monsters : from dragons to griffins / by Katie Marsico.
Description: Minneapolis : Lerner Publications, [2017] | Audience: Ages 7–11. | Audience: Grades 4
    to 6. | Includes bibliographical references and index.
Identifiers: LCCN 2016018570 (print) | LCCN 2016031645 (ebook) | ISBN 9781512425925 (lb : alk.
    paper) | ISBN 9781512428148 (eb pdf)
Subjects: LCSH: Dragons—Juvenile literature. | Griffins—Juvenile literature. | Animals, Mythical—
    Juvenile literature. | Animals, Mythical, in literature—Juvenile literature. | CYAC: Imaginary
    creatures.
Classification: LCC GR830.D7 M37 2017 (print) | LCC GR830.D7 (ebook) | DDC 398.24/54—dc23

LC record available at https://lccn.loc.gov/2016018570

Manufactured in the United States of America
1-41360-23304-6/29/2016

CONTENTS

INTRODUCTION
LARGER-THAN-LIFE LEGENDS

In medieval Europe, a powerful force made villagers tremble. It drove knights to go on dangerous journeys. And it let storytellers spin larger-than-life tales. This powerful force was the legend of dragons.

The dragons of medieval folklore were fierce. They breathed fire and had huge teeth. Sometimes they had spiked tails and wings. These dragons gobbled up humans and livestock. People saw them as symbols of evil.

Yet dragons are just one kind of beastly monster. What has the head of an eagle and the body of a lion? It's a griffin! And griffins are only one kind of hybrid monster. More modern tales of beastly monsters exist as well. They tell of Sasquatches and chupacabras.

Are these beasts real or imaginary? It's not always clear! Either way, they are the focus of lots of exciting stories and investigations.

A griffin has the wings and the head of an eagle and the legs of a lion.

Ancient Europeans believed dragons were wicked, scary creatures.

CHAPTER ONE
THE MAKINGS OF MONSTERS

Legends of beastly monsters began long ago. Dragon stories have been told for more than four thousand years! Think about the word *dragon*. It has roots in the Greek term *drakōn*. That means "serpent." Ancient Greeks probably used *drakōn* to describe large snakes. As time passed, mythology gave dragons a makeover.

People's location and religion shaped how they saw dragons. In Europe, these creatures were seen as wicked. Many Christians believed dragons stood for evil. In one Christian tale, Saint George kills a dragon. In this story, the beast represents the devil.

Killing a dragon took great courage. So people often preferred to avoid them. Some lit bonfires in the hopes of keeping dragons away. Others used herbs as dragon repellent.

Yet these beasts weren't always bad! Chinese storytellers described dragons as wise and generous. Some Chinese dragons resembled snakes and lizards. Others looked like lions or horses. In Chinese mythology, dragons breathed clouds. They controlled how water flowed. People honored them.

Blended Beasts

Many tales of hybrid monsters date back to the ancient world. People have told stories about griffins for thousands of years. Ancient peoples said these creatures guarded treasure. Griffins were considered strong and clever. Still, few people described them as friendly. They believed griffins became mean when threatened.

Dragons in ancient stories breathed fire and ate people for lunch.

Early cultures used storytelling and art to share ideas about beastly monsters. Dragons and hybrid beasts appeared in sculptures, paintings, and architecture. They also decorated ships, weapons, and shields. Some of these images still exist.

From Bigfoot to Bloodsuckers

Not every beastly monster is ancient. In the nineteenth century, settlers in the Pacific Northwest mentioned mysterious apelike beings. People called these hairy creatures Sasquatches. The name Sasquatch was first used by Coast Salish Indians. In English, it means "wild man." Sasquatches supposedly left huge footprints. These tracks earned them the nickname Bigfoot. Sometimes Sasquatches were blamed for killing farm animals. Occasionally, they were said to attack humans. Most Sasquatch sightings occurred in remote areas.

Starting in the 1980s, rumors of another monster swirled. They spread in Central and South America and the southwestern United States. Such stories began when farmers found animals dead—and drained of blood!

Some blamed a beast called the chupacabra. (That's Spanish for "goat sucker.") Those claiming to have seen chupacabras painted a vivid picture! Many said they resembled hairless dogs, large rats, kangaroos, or reptiles. Common features included red eyes and fangs. People believed chupacabras used their fangs to feed on victims' blood.

Some say they have proof of chupacabras and Sasquatches. Their evidence includes photos and videos. It also features hair samples and what are supposedly monster corpses. Of course, not everyone agrees on what these items actually show.

The first official report
of a chupacabra sighting
came from Puerto Rico.

VO STERS WHERE!

Beastly monsters were a big deal thousands of years ago. Since then, they've made it to Hollywood! Movies show these creatures are still part of pop culture. Special effects bring monsters to life on-screen. Sometimes films say dragons are misunderstood—and even cute! Examples include Disney's *How to Train Your Dragon* movies. These films feature a Viking boy named Hiccup and Toothless, a young dragon. The two develop a friendship. In turn, the Vikings find that not all dragons are monsters.

Hiccup and Toothless were so popular that they later starred in *How to Train Your Dragon 2*.

Other movies make a different statement. *The Hobbit* films and *Maleficent* feature fire-breathing dragons. These creatures are feared and hated.

In *Maleficent*, Angelina Jolie plays a villain who can transform into a fierce dragon.

Many fantastical monsters appear on TV as well. The Italian cartoon *Winx Club* is set in a magical universe. Some characters take the form of dragons. Others are alicorns, or winged unicorns.

From Reading to Roller Coasters

Books also show how beastly monsters fit into pop culture. One example is J. K. Rowling's Harry Potter series. Wizard Harry Potter lives alongside many amazing creatures. These include different types of dragons. Rowling introduces hybrids such as hippogriffs too. In mythology, hippogriffs are a blend of a griffin and a horse.

Beastly monsters inspire games and sports teams as well. Nintendo's *The Legend of Zelda* series includes dragons. So do the role-playing game *Dungeons & Dragons* and the card-trading game *Yu-Gi-Oh!* Meanwhile, hockey fans might recognize Griff. He's the mascot of the Grand Rapids Griffins.

Toy stores offer more proof of beastly monsters' popularity. Fans of Monster High dolls are probably familiar with Jinafire Long and Manny Taur. Jinafire is the daughter of two Chinese dragons, and Manny is a Minotaur. In Greek mythology, a Minotaur had a bull's head and a man's body.

Even amusement parks include beastly monsters. Visitors to Disney World's Animal Kingdom learn about yetis. Some think these creatures are similar to Sasquatches. Yet yetis live in South Asia's Himalaya mountain range. Expedition Everest is a roller coaster that features a robotic yeti measuring 25 feet (7.6 meters) tall. The ride makes thrill-seekers feel as if the yeti is chasing them through the Himalayas!

WHAT DO YOU THINK?

Do you think beastly monsters play a part in modern holidays or parties? Head online or visit the library. Search for pictures of Chinese New Year parades. Do you notice any familiar monsters? Did you know some towns hold chupacabra festivals? Try to find more examples of traditions involving such creatures. Do you think it's possible to both fear and celebrate certain ideas?

A chupacabra dances in a Dominican Day Parade in Brooklyn, New York.

17

Fossils of the dinosaur protoceratops may have inspired ancient tales of griffins.

CHAPTER THREE
MYTHS OR SOMETHING MORE?

Most stories of beastly monsters mix fact and fantasy. Real animals probably inspired early images of dragons. Some people may have assumed cobras, crocodiles, and lizards were mythological creatures.

And dinosaur fossils seemed to prove that such beasts were real. More than two thousand years ago, miners found protoceratops fossils in Asia's Gobi Desert. These men already believed that fierce griffins guarded the gold they were digging. To them, the fossils showed they were right!

In turn, miners may have relied on the bones to describe griffins. Like a lion, protoceratops walked on four legs. Like an eagle, it had a curved beak. This dinosaur's shoulder blades looked similar to wings. People used the remains of protoceratops to piece together a picture of a legend!

Apes and Aliens

What about Sasquatches? Cryptozoologists work to either prove or disprove the existence of beastly monsters. Some of them say monsters may be creatures that scientists have yet to identify. Or Sasquatches could be animals that were supposedly extinct. Or maybe they are a type of huge ape or early human.

There are also many possible explanations for chupacabras. Some say they're aliens' pets. Others think they're the product of a top-secret government experiment. Maybe scientists were trying to make a hybrid of multiple species. Chupacabras could be the result of lab work gone wrong! Finally, chupacabras might be a mysterious new animal. Until recently, it's possible they simply went unnoticed.

Other Explanations

Many people say there are scientific explanations for Sasquatches and chupacabras. Some sightings are mistaken identity. Witnesses may think they're seeing Sasquatches. Yet they might really be looking at black bears. Other people claim to find strands of Sasquatch hair.

Do you think Sasquatches are real? Or is there a scientific explanation for them?

Scientists examine the DNA in the hair. It usually traces to humans, bears, raccoons, deer, or dogs.

Scientists studying chupacabras have reached similar conclusions. Sometimes people report capturing or killing one of these creatures. But the "monster" almost always ends up being a raccoon or wild dog.

Sometimes evidence of monsters is a hoax, or trick. People create fake pictures and videos. These people want money or attention. They try to fool others with fake monster corpses and gorilla costumes! Yet a few fakers don't necessarily make beastly monsters less real. To many people, other explanations don't disprove that Sasquatches and chupacabras still lurk somewhere in the shadows.

A photo from a Sasquatch sighting can draw a lot of attention, whether it's real or not.

A CAREER IN CRYPTOZOOLOGY

Do you want to explore the unknown? Maybe you should become a cryptozoologist! Start by reading books and articles about the unknown. Then study animal or life science in college. But be aware of the downsides to this job! Cryptozoologists often pay for their own research. They also often work in far-off

places. And it's not always easy for cryptozoologists to convince others of their findings. Of course, cryptozoology can be very rewarding. It comes with opportunities for travel and adventure. And what's better than being able to say you solved a monster mystery?

Cryptologists look for monster clues, such as this cast of a footprint. Was it really from a Sasquatch?

CHAPTER FOUR
LIKELY TO LIVE ON

In the future, people will probably learn more about beastly monsters. Perhaps a future fossil dig will provide evidence of a dragon legend. Or maybe new technology will help scientists say for sure whether Sasquatches are an unidentified species.

Scientists are always improving how they study evidence such as DNA. This will help separate myths and misunderstandings from what is perhaps something more.

Thousands of years in the making, many beastly monsters are at the center of old legends. Others are the focus of modern mysteries. Such mysteries may remain unsolved for centuries to come. Yet beastly monsters tend to stick around in people's imaginations. Both terrible and terrific, they will likely live on forever.

Scientists may someday find fossil evidence of fire-breathing dragons.

GRIFFIN

SIZE

Comparable to a sheep

FIERCE FEATURES

Strength, smarts, wings, sharp beak, and claws

METHOD OF ATTACK

Rips apart flesh with beak and claws

LIKELY TO WIN OR LOSE

Likely to win

CHUPACABRA

SIZE
No larger than a medium-size dog

FIERCE FEATURES
Sharp teeth and fangs, incredible speed, and ability to hunt at night

METHOD OF ATTACK
Breaks skin and drains blood

LIKELY TO WIN OR LOSE
Likely to lose

GLOSSARY

corpses: dead bodies

DNA: a substance that carries genetic information in the cells of plants and animals. DNA stands for deoxyribonucleic acid.

fossils: the hardened remains of plants or animals

hybrid: the offspring of two or more different species

livestock: farm animals

mascot: an animal that brings good luck, especially when it represents a sports team

medieval: describing the Middle Ages, or the period from about 500 to 1500

pop culture: activities or products that show what's popular among big groups of people

remote: far from cities

repellent: something that keeps away insects or other animals seen as pests

FURTHER INFORMATION

Books

Flitcroft, Jean. *The Chupacabra*. Minneapolis: Darby Creek, 2014.

Peebles, Alice. *Demons and Dragons*. Minneapolis: Hungry Tomato™, 2016.

Smith, Roland. *Chupacabra*. New York: Scholastic, 2013.

Movies

DreamWorks Dragons. Broadcast 2012–2014, season 1–2, on Cartoon Network and 2015–, season 3–, on Netflix.

How to Train Your Dragon. Directed by Dean DeBlois. Glendale, CA: DreamWorks Animation / Mad Hatter Entertainment / Vertigo Entertainment, 2010.

Maleficent. Directed by Kenneth Branagh. Burbank, CA: Walt Disney Pictures / Roth Films, 2014.

TV Shows

Finding Bigfoot. Broadcast 2011– on Animal Planet.

"Texas: Lake Worth Monster (Goat Man), Chupacabra, Zombie Soldiers." *Monsters and Mysteries in America*. Broadcast December 15, 2013, on the Discovery Channel.

Winx Club. Directed by Iginio Straffi. Broadcast on Rai 2 and Rai Gulp in Italy and aired in other countries, 2004–.

Video Games

How to Train Your Dragon 2. Video game. Bayswater, Australia: Torus Games, 2014.

The Legend of Zelda: Tri Force Heroes. Video game. Redmond, WA: Nintendo Entertainment / Grezzo, 2015.

Lego: The Hobbit. Video game. Cheshire, UK: Traveller's Tales / TT Fusion, 2014.

Websites

Discovery Kids—Finding Bigfoot
http://discoverykids.com/games/finding-bigfoot/

KidzWorld—El Chupacabra
http://www.kidzworld.com/article/2151-el-chupacabra

National Geographic Kids—Five Terrifying Tales from Ancient Greek Mythology
http://www.ngkids.co.uk/history/Greek-Myths

LERNER

SOURCE

Expand learning beyond the printed book. Download free, complementary educational resources for this book from our website, www.lerneresource.com.

INDEX

PHOTO ACKNOWLEDGMENTS

The images in this book are used with the permission of:
© iStockphoto.com/South_agency, p. 1 (eyeball); © iStockphoto.
com/Natalia Lukiyanova, pp. 1, 2 (monster claws); © iStockphoto.
com/Lynne Yoshii (burnt parchment background); © iStockphoto.
com/konradlew (paper background edge); © iStockphoto.com/
STILLFX (red wall background); © iStockphoto.com/dmilovanovic,
pp. 2–3 (ripped paper edge); © Vuk Kostic/Shutterstock.com, pp.
4–5; © iStockphoto.com/cosmin4000, pp. 6–7; © iStockphoto.com/
fotokostic, pp. 8, 24–25; © iStockphoto.com/Alexander Chernyakov,
pp. 8–9 (fire background); © Jaime Chirinos/Science Source, pp.
10–11; Dreamworks Animation/The Kobal Collection/Art Resource,
NY, pp. 12–13; Dreamworks Animation/Mad Hatter Entertainment/
The Kobal Collection/Art Resource, NY, p. 13; Walt Disney Studios/
The Kobal Collection/Art Resource, NY, p. 14; © iStockphoto.com/
PopoudinaSvetlana, pp. 14–15 (landscape background); © iStockphoto.
com/Kevin Landwer-Johan, pp. 16–17; © Citizen of the Planet/
SuperStock, p. 17 (chupacabra dancer); © iStockphoto.com/Adam
Smigielski, pp. 17, 23 (red grunge background); © AntoninJury/
Wikimedia Commons (CC BY-SA 4.0), pp. 18–19; © Buddy Mays/
Alamy, pp. 20–21; © Russ Kinne/Animals Animals, p. 22; ©
iStockphoto.com/Christopher-Lee, pp. 22–23 (forest background); AP
Photo/Jim Salter, p. 23; © Ralf Juergen Kraft/Shutterstock.com, p. 26;
© iStockphoto.com/AVTG, pp. 26–27 (forest background); © Alexlky/
Shutterstock.com, p. 27; © iStockphoto.com/Studio-Annika, pp. 28–29,
31, 32 (ripped paper edge).

Cover: © iStockphoto.com/AYDIN OZON (dragon); © iStockphoto.
com/South_agency (eyeball); © iStockphoto.com/Natalia Lukiyanova
(monster claws); © iStockphoto.com/ Lynne Yoshii (burnt parchment);
© iStockphoto.com/STILLFX (red wall background).